Biggest, Baddest Books for Boys

BIGGEST, BADDEST BOOK OF

PIRATES

ANDERS HANSON & KATHERINE HENGEL

Consulting Editor, Diane Craig, M.A./Reading Specialist

A Division of ABDO

ABDO
Publishing Company

visit us at www.abdopublishing.com

Published by ABDO Publishing Company, a division of ABDO, P.O. Box 398166, Minneapolis, Minnesota 55439. Copyright © 2013 by Abdo Consulting Group, Inc. International copyrights reserved in all countries. No part of this book may be reproduced in any form without written permission from the publisher. Super SandCastle™ is a trademark and logo of ABDO Publishing Company.

Printed in the United States of America, North Mankato, Minnesota
062012
092012

 PRINTED ON RECYCLED PAPER

Editor: Liz Salzmann
Content Developer: Nancy Tuminelly
Cover and Interior Design and Production: Anders Hanson, Mighty Media, Inc.
Illustration Credits: Shutterstock

Library of Congress Cataloging-in-Publication Data
Hanson, Anders, 1980-
  Biggest, baddest book of pirates / Anders Hanson and Katherine Hengel.
    p. cm. -- (Biggest, baddest books for boys)
  Audience: Ages 4-10.
  ISBN 978-1-61783-408-0 (alk. paper)
  1. Pirates--Juvenile literature. I. Hengel, Katherine. II. Title.
  G535.H265 2012
  910.4'5--dc23
                              2011050920

Super SandCastle™ books are created by a team of professional educators, reading specialists, and content developers around five essential components—phonemic awareness, phonics, vocabulary, text comprehension, and fluency—to assist young readers as they develop reading skills and strategies and increase their general knowledge. All books are written, reviewed, and leveled for guided reading, early reading intervention, and Accelerated Reader® programs for use in shared, guided, and independent reading and writing activities to support a balanced approach to literacy instruction.

CONTENTS

Ahoy, Matey! 4

How to Spot a Pirate 5

The Pirate Code 6

Chain of Command 7

Luck and Superstition 7

Infamous Pirates 8

Pirate Women 11

Grog and Gruel 12

Dangers of Pirate Life 13

Pirates to Arms! 14

Pirate Ships 16

The Jolly Roger 18

Pirate Treasure 20

Pirate Jokes 22

What Do Ye Know About Pirates? 23

Glossary 24

AHOY, MATEY!

Pirates Arrr Scallywags!

Want to learn about pirates? Be ye brave enough? Piracy is stealing on the high seas. The high seas are the open parts of the ocean. These waters aren't protected. They're perfect for pirates!

HOW TO SPOT A PIRATE

CAPTAIN'S HAT

EYE PATCH

BEARD

PISTOL

CAPTAIN'S JACKET

CUTLASS

TREASURE

Picture a pirate. What do you imagine? Treasure? Parrots? What about a peg leg?

These ideas come from movies and books. People love pirate stories! Some are true. Some are not.

THE PIRATE CODE

Arrr! Pirates broke a lot of laws. They made some up too!

Rule One

Every man votes and gets equal food and drink.

Rule Two

Lights and candles out at 8 P.M.

Rule Three

Keep your weapons clean and ready.

Rule Four

No kids or women on the ship.

Rule Five

Deserters will be killed.

Rule Six

No one takes more than his share!

CHAIN OF COMMAND

KNOW WHO IS IN CHARGE!

THE CAPTAIN leads the ship.

THE QUARTERMASTER hands out **gunpowder** and treasure.

THE BOATSWAIN assigns jobs to the crew.

THE GUNNER leads the men who fire the cannons.

THE CARPENTER fixes the ship.

THE COOK makes the meals.

SUPERSTITION

Pirates have a lot of **superstitions**! See if you know them all!

BAD LUCK

WHISTLING

Whistling is bad luck. One can "whistle up a storm"!

FRIDAY 13 FRIDAYS

Never set sail on a Friday. Friday the 13th is the worst!

LEFT FOOT FIRST

Never board a ship left foot first. Don't sneeze to the left either!

GOOD LUCK

CATS

Cats are good luck. If a cat goes overboard, a storm is coming!

MAGIC KNOTS

A thick rope with three knots brings good wind.

SEA LIFE

Gulls and dolphins are good luck. Don't hurt them!

7

BLACKBEARD

REAL NAME: *Edward Teach*

YEARS AS A PIRATE: *1716–1718*

LOCATION: *Atlantic Ocean*

SHIPS: *Queen Anne's Revenge, Adventure*

Blackbeard never used force. He didn't have to. Everyone was afraid of him! Blackbeard treated his crew well. Some say he never hurt his prisoners.

PIRATES

CAPTAIN KIDD

REAL NAME: *William Kidd*

YEARS AS A PIRATE: *1689–1701*

LOCATION: *Caribbean Sea, Red Sea, Indian Ocean*

SHIPS: *Blessed William, Antigua, Adventure Galley*

Captain Kidd stole from French ships. But he wasn't a pirate! He was a **privateer** for Great Britain. Some say he became a pirate in 1697. A British court found him guilty in 1701.

BLACK BART

REAL NAMES: *John Roberts, Bartholomew Roberts*

YEARS AS A PIRATE: *1719–1722*

LOCATION: *Atlantic Ocean*

SHIPS: *Royal Fortune, Ranger, Little Ranger, Good Fortune, Royal Rover, Puerto del Principe*

Black Bart worked near the Americas and West Africa. He was very successful. He attacked 470 ships!

CALICO JACK

REAL NAME: *John Rackham*

YEARS AS A PIRATE: *1717–1720*

LOCATION: *Caribbean Sea*

SHIPS: *Treasure, Kingston, Revenge*

Calico Jack did things his way. He robbed small ships close to shore. It was risky!

He was hanged in 1720.

PIRATE WOMEN

Most captains didn't let women on board. But Calico Jack did! These **hardy** lassies were in his crew!

Anne Bonny

YEARS AS A PIRATE: *1718–1720*

LOCATION: *Caribbean Sea*

SHIPS: *Revenge*

Anne Bonny married young. Her husband just wanted her father's money. Bonny met Calico Jack in the Bahamas. She left her husband and became a pirate!

Mary Read

YEARS AS A PIRATE: *1709–1720*

LOCATION: *Caribbean Sea*

SHIPS: *Revenge*

Mary Read joined Calico Jack in 1720. His ship was caught that year. Read was sent to trial. But only Jack was hanged.

GROG & GRUEL

Pirates sailed for weeks at a time. They kept fresh water in barrels. But water spoils. Yuck! So pirates added lime juice and **spirits**.

Their food spoiled too. It was full of bugs! They ate at night. They didn't want to see their food!

BATHROOM BREAK!

Most pirates had no bathroom. They had to go off the side of the ship!

HARDTACK

Hardtack is a biscuit. It's made from flour, water, and salt.

GRUEL

Gruel is made from boiled grains.

SALTED MEATS

Salt helps meat last longer.

FRESH FRUITS

Fruits were picked on shore.

GROG

Lime juice and spirits kept the water fresh.

SEA TURTLES

Sea turtles were kept on the ship until eaten.

DANGERS OF PIRATE LIFE

BEING A PIRATE SOUNDS COOL. BUT IT WASN'T ALL FUN AND GAMES!

DISEASE AND INJURY

Pirates had poor diets. They were often sick.

Doctors and medicines were rare. Injured limbs had to be cut off! That's how pirates stopped infections.

Pirates lived on the water. But most couldn't swim. Many drowned.

DEADLY PUNISHMENT

The pirate code was strict. Pirates who broke it were often killed. Or they were left on deserted islands.

CUTLASS

A cutlass is a short sword.
It has a curved blade.

PIRATES

BLUNDERBUSS

This is a gun with a short barrel. It is loaded
with **gunpowder** and lead balls.

PISTOL

Pistols are fired with one hand.
Their range is short.

GRENADE

Grenades are
filled with
gunpowder.
They have
fuses inside.

MUSKET

Muskets are long guns. Their range is
50 to 100 yards (45 to 90 m).

TO ARMS!

GOLDEN AGE OF PIRACY

GRAPPLING HOOK

Pirates used them to hook onto other ships.

CANNON

A cannon shoots cannonballs. Some cannonballs weigh up to 42 pounds (19 kg)!

RAPIER

A rapier is a skinny sword. It has a sharp point.

SWIVEL GUN

A swivel gun is a small cannon. It's on a stand that turns.

PIRATE SHIPS

SLOOP

SCHOONER

BARQUE

BRIGANTINE

WARSHIP

FRIGATE

Most pirate ships were stolen **merchant** ships. Merchant ships were huge. They could haul a lot of goods. Pirates stole these goods along with the ships.

Pirates liked fast ships with a lot of cannons.

16

MAINMAST

FOREMAST

MIZZEN MAST

SQUARE SAIL

LATEEN SAIL

SHROUDS

TOP

CAPTAIN'S QUARTERS

BOWSPRIT

AFT

ANCHOR

BOW

THE JOLLY ROGER

A Jolly Roger is a pirate flag. Pirates liked to design their own. Some have skulls. Others have hearts. Some are red. Others are black. But they are all Jolly Rogers!

SAM BELLAMY

CALICO JACK

WALTER KENNEDY

EDWARD LOW

BLACKBEARD

STEDE BONNET

Pirates didn't raise the Jolly Roger often. They only raised it when they were close enough to attack another ship. The Jolly Roger would scare the other crew. Sometimes they would give up without a fight!

THOMAS TEW

HENRY EVERY

CHRISTOPHER MOODY

BLACK BART I

BLACK BART II

RICHARD WORLEY

PIRATE TREASURE

CAPTAIN KIDD'S BURIED TREASURE

Captain Kidd was a wanted pirate! So he sailed to New York in 1699. He wanted to tell the governor he was innocent. It was his only choice.

Would the governor believe him? Kidd didn't know. So he buried his treasure! He hid it on an island near New York.

The governor found Kidd guilty. He sent him to England for trial. He dug up Kidd's treasure too. Kidd was hanged in 1701.

PIRATES LIVED FOR TREASURE. BUT THEY OFTEN LOST THEIR LOOT!

THE WRECK OF THE *WHYDAH*

A storm sank the *Whydah* near Cape Cod in 1717. It sank with almost five tons of treasure!

In 1984, underwater explorers found the ship. They also found coins, gold dust, and jewelry!

PIRATE JOKES

What has 12 arms, 12 legs, and 12 eyes? *A dozen pirates.*

Why did the pirate see a movie? *It was rated Arrr.*

Where did the one-legged pirate go for breakfast? *The IHOP.*

How much does it cost for a pirate to pierce his ears? *A buck an ear!*

Why did the pirate get his ship so cheaply? *Because it was on sail.*

Why does it take pirates so long to learn the alphabet? *Because they can spend years at C!*

WHAT DO YE KNOW ABOUT PIRATES?

1. PIRATES STEAL ON LAND. **TRUE OR FALSE?**

2. PIRATES MADE UP THEIR OWN LAWS. **TRUE OR FALSE?**

3. HARDTACK IS A TYPE OF MEAT. **TRUE OR FALSE?**

4. A JOLLY ROGER IS A PIRATE FLAG. **TRUE OR FALSE?**

ANSWERS: 1) FALSE   2) TRUE   3) FALSE   4) TRUE

23

GLOSSARY

DESERTER – someone who leaves a group or cause without permission and doesn't plan to return.

GUNPOWDER – a mixture of materials that explodes and is used in guns and cannons.

HARDY – strong and tough.

LOOT – things that have been stolen.

MERCHANT – having to do with trade, especially between different countries.

PRIVATEER – a person who has his or her country's permission to attack foreign ships.

SPIRITS – strong alcohol, such as whisky or gin.

SUPERSTITION – a belief that magic or luck can cause something to happen.